Spotted Beetles
Ladybugs in Your Backyard

Written by Nancy Loewen
Illustrated by Melissa Voda

Backyard Bugs

Thanks to our advisers for their expertise, research, knowledge, and advice:

Gary A. Dunn, M.S., Director of Education
Young Entomologists' Society
Lansing, Michigan

Susan Kesselring, M.A., Literacy Educator
Rosemount-Apple Valley-Eagan (Minnesota) School District

PICTURE WINDOW BOOKS
Minneapolis, Minnesota

Managing Editor: Bob Temple
Creative Director: Terri Foley
Editors: Nadia Higgins, Brenda Haugen
Editorial Adviser: Andrea Cascardi
Copy Editor: Laurie Kahn
Designer: Melissa Voda
Page production: Picture Window Books
The illustrations in this book were prepared digitally.

Picture Window Books
5115 Excelsior Boulevard
Suite 232
Minneapolis, MN 55416
1-877-845-8392
www.picturewindowbooks.com

Printed in the United States of America.

Library of Congress Cataloging-in-Publication Data
Loewen, Nancy, 1964–
Spotted beetles : ladybugs in your backyard / written by Nancy Loewen ; illustrated by
Melissa Voda.
p. cm. — (Backyard bugs)
Summary: Describes the physical characteristics, life cycle, and behavior of ladybugs.
Includes bibliographical references (p.   ) and index.
ISBN 1-4048-0142-1 (hard cover)
1. Ladybugs — Juvenile literature. [1. Ladybugs.] I. Melissa Voda, ill. II. Title.
QL596.C65L64 2003
595.76'9—dc21
                                                                 2003006090

Table of Contents

Bright Beetles

It's wonderful in the garden. Tiny cucumbers are forming on the vines. New tomatoes look like pale-green marbles. Spiky onion tops bend in the breeze.

The best part is, if you look closely, you can see a whole world of tiny creatures.

4

Look at that potato plant. Little spotted domes are moving slowly over its leaves. You know what they are. Ladybugs!

It's fun to watch ladybugs fly. One second there's a tiny black blur in the air. Then suddenly there's a bright beetle crawling around. Here comes another one!

There are 5,000 kinds of ladybugs. Most are orange, red, or yellow, but some are white or black. Not all species have spots. The convergent ladybug is the kind described in this book. It is the most common ladybug found in North America.

What Do Ladybugs Eat?

It looks like the ladybugs aren't
the only bugs visiting the potato plant.
Those tiny green insects are aphids.
They're also called plant lice.

Aphids are a ladybug's favorite food.

By eating aphids and other small insects, ladybugs keep plants healthier. In fact, people often buy ladybugs to get rid of pests in the garden.

What Happens to Ladybug Eggs?

What are those tiny yellow beads under that leaf?
They're probably ladybug eggs. Ladybugs lay
their eggs where there are lots of aphids.
The eggs will hatch in three to five days.

What comes out of a ladybug egg? It doesn't look like a ladybug. It's a larva. Look! There are some on that leaf. They look like hungry little alligators.

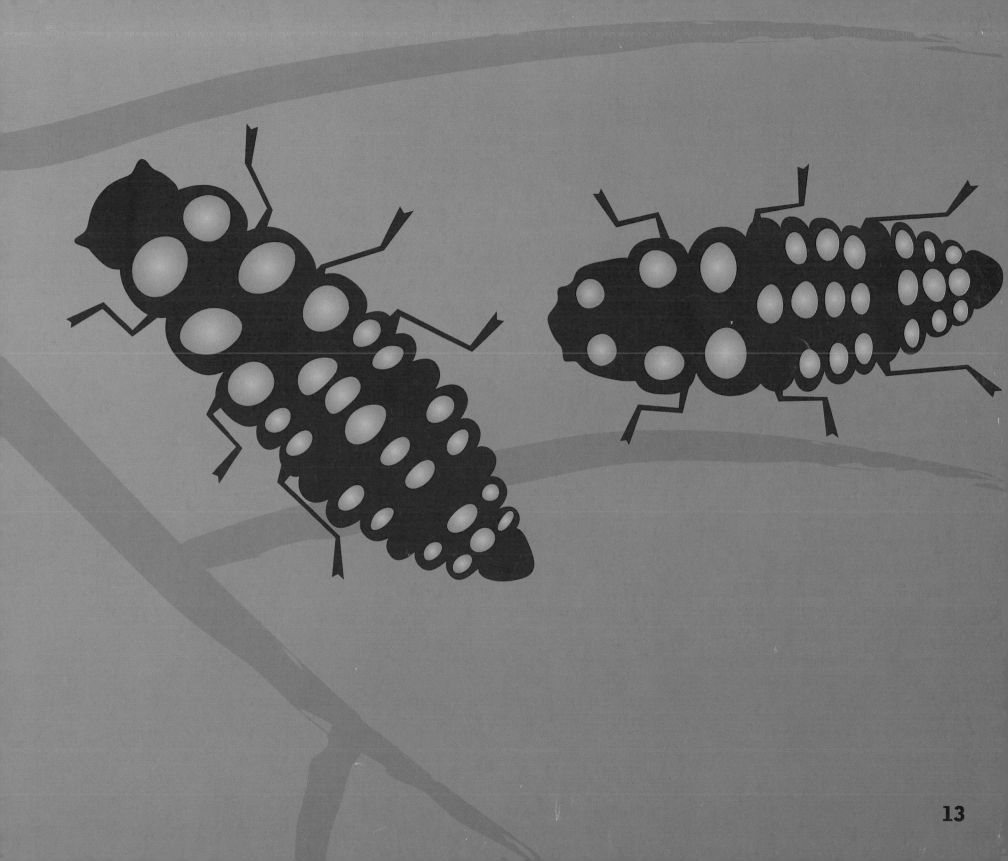

A larva will eat aphids and other small insects. It will grow for three to four weeks. Then it will stick its body to the bottom of a leaf, and a shell will form around it. It will become a pupa.

Here's one. It looks a little like a bird dropping, doesn't it? But in 7 to 10 days, a new ladybug will come out of it.

New ladybugs don't have spots. It takes a day or so for their spots to appear.

How Long Do Ladybugs Live?

Most adult ladybugs live for a few weeks to a few months.
Some ladybugs that hatch in early autumn live much longer.
They find a hidden place and sleep all winter. Then, in the spring,
they mate and the females lay eggs. The life cycle starts all over again.

Ladybugs often end up
indoors for the winter.
They find a quiet place to
sleep but might wake up
on a sunny day.

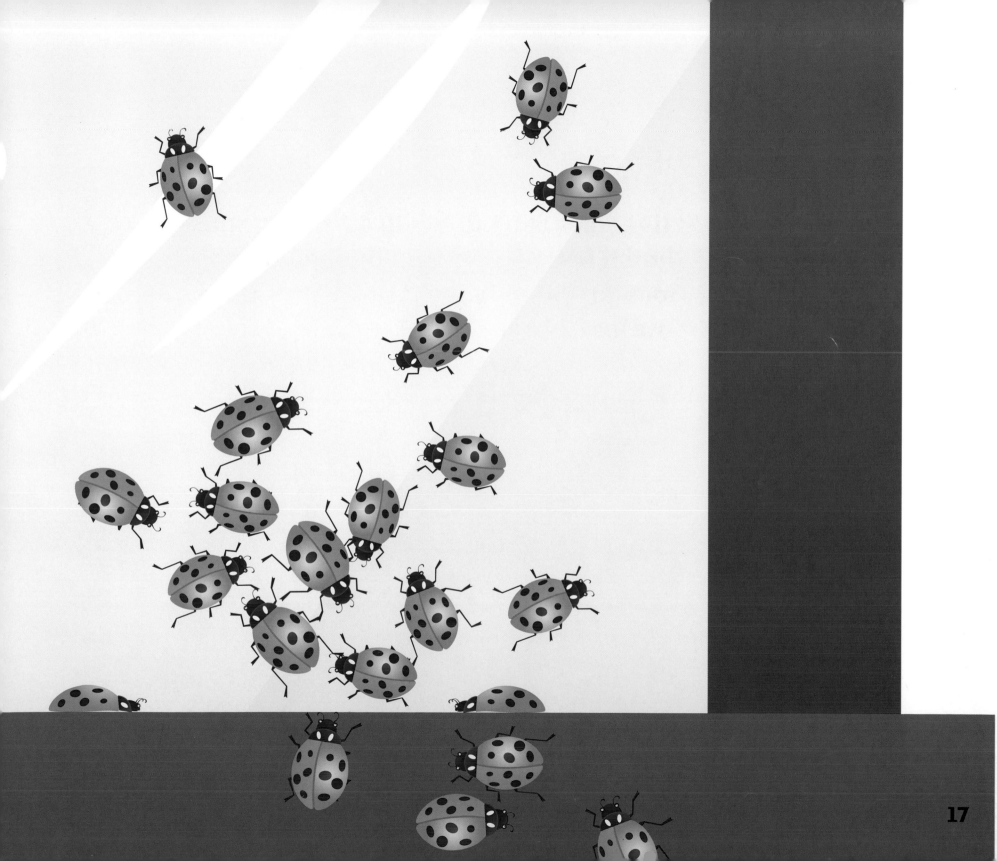

Tricky Bugs

Here's a ladybug on its back with its legs folded in.
Is it dead? Maybe, but it might be pretending to be dead.
That's one way ladybugs keep from being bothered
by other animals. Bigger insects, toads, and birds
sometimes eat ladybugs—but they don't like to eat
ladybugs that already are dead.

A ladybug's bright color also keeps it safe. The color is a sign to enemies that the ladybug doesn't taste good.

A Friend in the Garden

It looks like this one is alive after all. And see? It likes you!

Look Closely at a Ladybug

Look at a ladybug through a magnifying glass.
How many of these different parts can you see?

A ladybug uses **antennae** to touch, smell, and taste.
The **pronotum** helps to hide and protect the head.
Hard outer wings protect the body.
Soft wings underneath are for flying.
Like all insects, a ladybug has six **legs**.

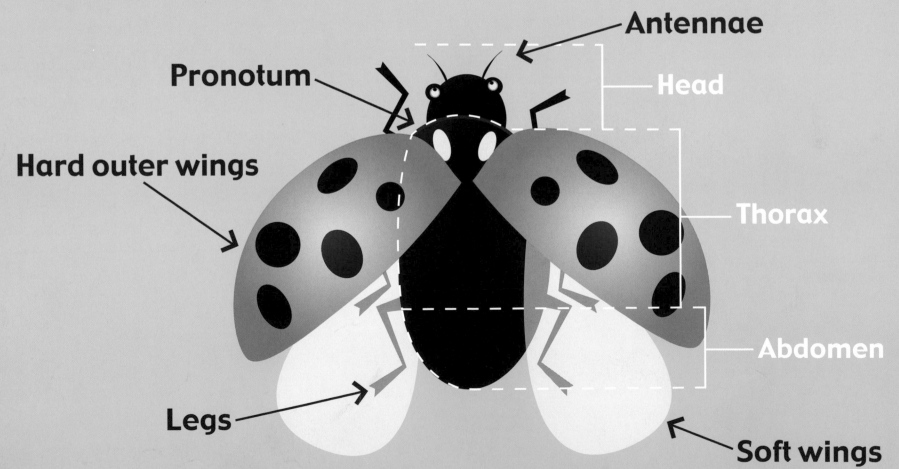

Antennae

Pronotum

Head

Hard outer wings

Thorax

Abdomen

Legs

Soft wings

Fun Facts

- In some countries, people believe ladybugs bring good luck. In England, finding a ladybug means there will be a good harvest. In France, ladybugs mean good health. In Sweden, if a ladybug lands on a young woman's hand, it means she will soon be married.

- A ladybug might eat more than 5,000 aphids in its lifetime.

- The ladybug is the official state insect of Delaware, Massachusetts, New Hampshire, Ohio, and Tennessee.

- Ladybugs that are sold to gardeners or farmers are measured by gallons. One gallon (four liters) holds up to 80,000 ladybugs!

- When flying, a ladybug flaps its wings 85 times per second.

Make a Ladybug Rhyme

Here is a very old nursery rhyme about ladybugs:

Ladybug! Ladybug! Fly away home.
Your house is on fire, your children all gone.
All but one, and her name is Ann,
And she crept under the pudding pan.

This rhyme was told hundreds of years ago. After the harvest, people burned their fields to clear them. The ladybugs would fly away, leaving the larvae and pupae.

Make up your own rhyme about ladybugs. Start by saying what you like most about ladybugs.

Words to Know

aphids–Aphids (AY-fids) are tiny green insects that ladybugs eat.

larva–A newly hatched ladybug is called a larva. A larva looks like a tiny alligator. Larvae (LAR-vee) is the word for more than one larva.

life cycle–A life cycle is the series of changes that take place in a living thing, from birth to death.

mate–Male and female ladybugs mate by joining together special parts of their bodies. After they've mated, the female can lay eggs.

pronotum–The pronotum is the part of a ladybug that helps hide and protect the ladybug's head.

pupa–A pupa (PYOO-puh) is a ladybug that is changing from a larva to an adult. These changes take place in a cocoon, or case.

To Learn More

At the Library

Allen, Judy. *Are You a Ladybug?* New York: Kingfisher, 2000.

Carle, Eric. *The Grouchy Ladybug.* New York: HarperCollins, 1996.

Heinrichs, Ann. *Ladybugs.* Minneapolis: Compass Point Books, 2002.

Posada, Mia. *Ladybugs: Red, Fiery, and Bright.* Minneapolis: Carolrhoda Books, Inc., 2002.

On the Web

enature.com
http://www.enature.com/guides/select_Insects_and_Spiders.asp
Articles about and photos of almost 300 species of insects and spiders

The National Park Service
http://www1.nature.nps.gov/wv/insects.htm
A guide to finding and studying insects at national parks

University of Kentucky Department of Entomology
http://www.uky.edu/Agriculture/Entomology/ythfacts/entyouth.htm
A kid-friendly site with insect games, jokes, articles, and resources

Fact Hound
Fact Hound offers a safe, fun way to find Web sites related to this book. All of the sites on Fact Hound have been researched by our staff.
http://www.facthound.com

1. Visit the Fact Hound home page.

2. Enter a search word related to this book, or type in this special code: 1404801421.

3. Click on the FETCH IT button.

Your trusty Fact Hound will fetch the best sites for you!